Ranching in the Great American Desert

★ ★ ★

by Patty North

Scott Foresman
is an imprint of

Glenview, Illinois • Boston, Massachusetts • Chandler, Arizona
Upper Saddle River, New Jersey

ISBN 13: 978-0-328-51638-4
ISBN 10:   0-328-51638-4

4 5 6 7 8 9 10 V0FL 14 13 12 11

Government worker Stephen Long drew a map in 1823 that showed a region called the "Great American Desert." This region contained much of what is now part of the United States between the Missouri River and the Rocky Mountains. Few people had seen the area for themselves, so they believed the map. Explorer Zebulon Pike thought the area was unfit for farming, and he thought the land should be left for the native people who lived there.

The Great American Desert

The writer Washington Irving traveled only as far as Missouri and Arkansas before giving his opinion of the area and points west. He said that it was a barren land without trees and with lots of sand. He also noted that no one lived there permanently because in certain seasons no food could be found.

Pioneers traveling westward already knew that good land awaited settlement on the far west coast. They hurried as quickly as their slow and heavy wagon trains would take them, across the country into what is now Utah, Oregon, and California.

Washington Irving (left)

A covered wagon crosses the plains (below).

The land in present-day Colorado, Wyoming, Kansas, parts of Nebraska and other states was thought to be too dry and useless for farming. Most people preferred to leave it to the Native Americans who lived there, as well as the Eastern Native American nations who had been relocated there by the U.S. government. These Native Americans survived by hunting the buffalo that roamed through the grasslands.

The wild and dry land was good enough for the people planning railroads, however. People saw that there was a need for better transportation across the region to reach California. The railroad developers could buy this barren land cheaply.

The Plains Indians used every part of the buffalo they hunted. From the buffalo, they got their food, clothing, and material for making shelters.

President Abraham Lincoln wanted to connect all parts of the United States, from the Atlantic to the Pacific. In 1862 he asked Congress, the selected group of people that makes laws for the country, to approve plans for a transcontinental railway.

Around this time, some settlers discovered that parts of the "Great American Desert" were actually useful for farming, even though the area didn't get much rain. The railroad companies encouraged people to buy the land that lay along the tracks from the railroad. The "Great American Desert" was renamed the "Great Plains."

Colorful posters were used to advertise the new Transcontinental Railroad in 1869.

Meanwhile, cattle ranching, which was brought to Mexico by Spanish explorers in the 1500s, was spreading into Texas and other parts of the western United States. Cattle ranchers needed a way to reach the markets of the big eastern cities. At first that seemed impossible—but then, in the 1860s, along came the railroads, which could carry the cattle farther east.

Ranchers guided their herds on a "long drive" across one thousand miles of mostly empty plains. Then, in railroad towns such as Abilene, Kansas, cowboys herded the cattle into freight cars headed for Chicago, Illinois. From there, the cattle were butchered and the meat was shipped to the rest of the country.

Chicago was once the meatpacking capital of the country.

Most cattle herders followed one of several trails to reach the railroad towns. The trails had names such as the Goodnight-Loving Trail and the Shawnee Trail. One famous trail was the Chisholm Trail, which started near San Antonio, Texas, and continued north through Oklahoma, ending in Abilene, Kansas. Between 1867 and 1884, four million cattle were driven along this trail.

The men who traveled the Chisholm Trail were called "cowboys." The life of a cowboy was a very hard life. A long drive could last three or four months. Cowboys were often on horseback for eighteen hours a day. The heat and the dust kicked up by the huge herds made the cowboys' job uncomfortable. A large herd could be as much as a mile or more in length.

Driving a herd of cattle was dangerous work too. Sometimes cowboys had to cross rivers while their herds were **bawling** loudly. Thunderstorms often spooked the cattle into stampeding. A stampede is a sudden rush of panic-stricken animals.

★ ✖ ★

The wild rush could hurt or kill cattle and cowboys alike. Cowboys rode among the cattle, trying to keep the herd together, but often an animal broke away. Then a cowboy would have to rope it and bring it back.

After reaching the railroad towns, cowboys herded cattle into freight cars.

The Texas longhorn was the hardest to handle. This animal had sharp horns that could span seven feet, and it might weigh twelve hundred pounds. The Texas longhorn's toughness helped it survive the long journey. However, its meat could be as tough and stringy as its character.

Some TV shows and movies make the life of a cowboy seem attractive as well as exciting. They show cowboys galloping along or singing around evening campfires while a **coyote** howls. Not often do they show the reality of the cowboys' hard work and lonely life on the plains.

Look at the pointed horns!

From the Mexican *vaqueros,* or cattle-drivers, cowboys learned riding and roping. They also adopted the Mexican equipment of saddles, **spurs,** chaps, and lassos, or ropes.

The small towns, or "cow towns," that grew up quickly along the cattle trails were lawless places. Often there were no law officials to keep the peace. Cowboys could easily get into trouble in those wild places. They also had to keep track of their pay. A cowboy's pay might be only about one dollar a day.

About one-third of the cowboys were African American or Mexican.

Cattle ranching could be quite good for those who owned ranches. Ranchers grazed their cattle, or put them out to feed, on open ranges that belonged to the government. This way, ranchers didn't have to buy feed. The free-roaming cattle were so fierce and wild that it was dangerous to approach them on foot or without a weapon for protection. The only animal on the plains that was more dangerous was the grizzly bear.

When the grass was used up, ranchers moved on to new land. Early ranches might be simply a dugout shelter and a horse corral. Ranchers didn't even have to hire many workers until it was time for a **roundup.** Then the cattle were gathered into a herd to drive to market.

Cattle graze on the open range.

As settlers continued to set up farms on the plains, they had problems with the ranchers. Farmers needed grassland and water for the sheep they raised. They also wanted to keep cattle out of their crops. Driving cattle to the railroads became more difficult when cowboys had to keep their herds from trampling through farmers' fields.

The invention of barbed wire in 1874 gave the farmers an advantage. By stringing the sharp-pointed wire around their property, farmers could keep out the ranchers' cattle. Sometimes ranchers used wire cutters to make way for their cattle.

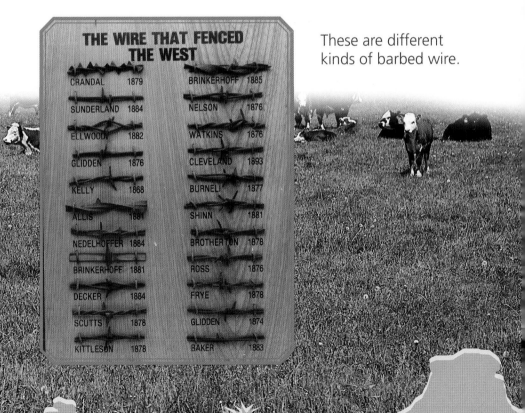

THE WIRE THAT FENCED THE WEST

CRANDAL	1879	BRINKERHOFF	1885
SUNDERLAND	1884	NELSON	1876
ELLWOOD	1882	WATKINS	1876
GLIDDEN	1876	CLEVELAND	1893
KELLY	1868	BURNELL	1877
ALLIS	1881	SHINN	1881
NEDELHOFFER	1884	BROTHERTON	1878
BRINKERHOFF	1881	ROSS	1876
DECKER	1884	FRYE	1878
SCUTTS	1878	GLIDDEN	1874
KITTLESON	1878	BAKER	1883

These are different kinds of barbed wire.

By 1886 the price of cattle had fallen to $10 each, down from $30. In addition, two extremely cold winters with blinding blizzards killed many cattle. Ranchers began moving farther westward to stay in business, and as they moved, their places were taken over by farmers. The great era of the cattle industry had lasted only about twenty years.

Ranch life, however, still exists today, and it is still tough. Ranchers struggle against the weather. The grass that they need to feed their cattle will not grow without rain, so ranchers often raise crops. Irrigation ditches that channel water from rivers keep these crops watered.

These cattle are stranded in a blizzard.

The seasons of the year control the work of ranchers. In the spring, they turn out the cattle, including the newborn calves, to graze. The ranchers brand the calves at this time. Red-hot iron markers are used to burn away part of the calves' hair and leave the particular mark that belongs to each ranch. During the summer, ranchers move their cattle from one area to another as the grass is used up.

Summer is also the season for rodeos, where audiences can watch cowboys show the skills they use in their everyday work. They demonstrate how quickly they can rope and tie a calf, as well as how long they can stay in the saddle on a bucking horse. Other events are bull riding and bareback riding, in which cowboys ride a horse without a saddle.

Cowboys show their skills at a rodeo.

Kids who live on ranches look forward to the fairs held during the summer. At the fairs, young people show the projects they have worked on all year. Some kids raise cattle, while others prefer sheep, pigs, or even rabbits. They all hope to win a blue ribbon.

In the late fall, the cattle feed on the last of the grasses on the plains. Autumn can come to a sudden end on the plains, with cold weather and snow sweeping in.

In winter, ranchers bring their cattle back from the grazing fields and feed them hay near the ranch house. Some cattle are sold and sent off to market, often by truck. Winter is also the time to catch up on chores around a ranch. During these slower days, ranchers make plans for the next season. They worry about the weather to come and the cattle prices.

To add to their income, some ranches invite paying guests to vacation on their land. People from cities who are unfamiliar with horses and ranch life are called **dudes.** These visitors take part in bringing cattle together in roundups and other ranch chores.

To get hands-on experience with activities related to ranching, many young people from the ages of ten to twenty-one take part in 4-H clubs. The four H's in *4-H* stand for head, heart, hands, and health. Members of these clubs take part in agricultural activities, including caring for horses and other animals. Some clubs even offer members a chance to work with cattle.

By working with animals, young people in 4-H clubs learn a lot, gain new skills, and sometimes even win a ribbon.

In the twenty-first century, there are fewer small family ranches and more large ones owned by big companies. A huge problem for ranches of all sizes is the water supply. As cities grow on the plains, the people living there need more water. The water in local rivers and under the ground has to be shared by more and more people.

Some plains residents worry about desertification, which means "turning into desert." No one wants to see the southwestern part of the United States actually become the "Great American Desert" that mapmakers once mistakenly described.

Keeping a steady water supply is a problem for many ranches.

This is a rolling irrigation system.

Glossary

bawling *v.* shouting or crying in a noisy way.

coyote *n.* a small, wolflike mammal living in many parts of North America.

dudes *n.* in the western parts of the United States and Canada, people raised in the city, especially easterners who vacation on a ranch.

roundup *n.* the act of driving or bringing cattle together from long distances.

spurs *n.* metal points or pointed wheels worn on a rider's boot heel for urging a horse on.